whisper essential friend

by

cmlehane

First published by Author House 12/30/04

Cover design by Marilyn Granald

Certificate of Registration
Number TXu 1-158-914
The Library of Congress
Copyright Office
101 Independence Ave., S.E.
Washington D.C. 20559-6000

ISBN: 1-4208-0434-0 (sc)

Library of Congress Control Number: 2004099213

Printed in the United States of America
Bloomington, IN

This book is printed on acid free paper.

authorHOUSE

1663 LIBERTY DRIVE
BLOOMINGTON, INDIANA 47403
(800) 839-8640
www.authorhouse.com

for kath

colleen's psalm

out of the depths
i cry to you
oh lord *

the depths of despair
the depths of loneliness
the depths of fear
the depths of desire

Unspeakable grief
Unspeakable things
sins of the flesh.
confusion
terror
torture
torment

separated by death
separated by fault
separated by sin
time
distance
uncertainty
loyalty
fidelity
betrayal

* psalm 130:1

you are the lord
the god of all people
*is anything too hard for you? ***

heal our broken hearts
mend our wounded souls
reconcile us to you
and to each other

take the desires of our hearts
and let them honor you
and in doing so
honor each other

i beg you, sweet jesus,
answer my prayer

02/2002

* jeremiah 32:27

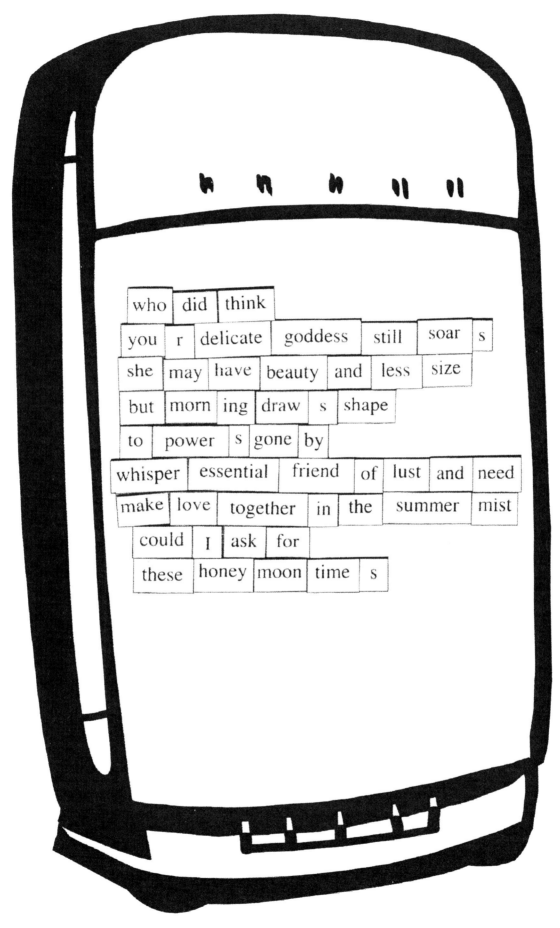

who did think
you r delicate goddess still soar s
she may have beauty and less size
but morn ing draw s shape
to power s gone by
whisper essential friend of lust and need
make love together in the summer mist
could I ask for
these honey moon time s

I don't think
We do too well
Over the telephone
As time goes by

You're always tired
When you call
And I go brain dead
Caught in a free fall

Then, something you said
Sticks in my head
For days
And even more

Until you call again
And even then
You're so tired
And I go brain dead

07/1997

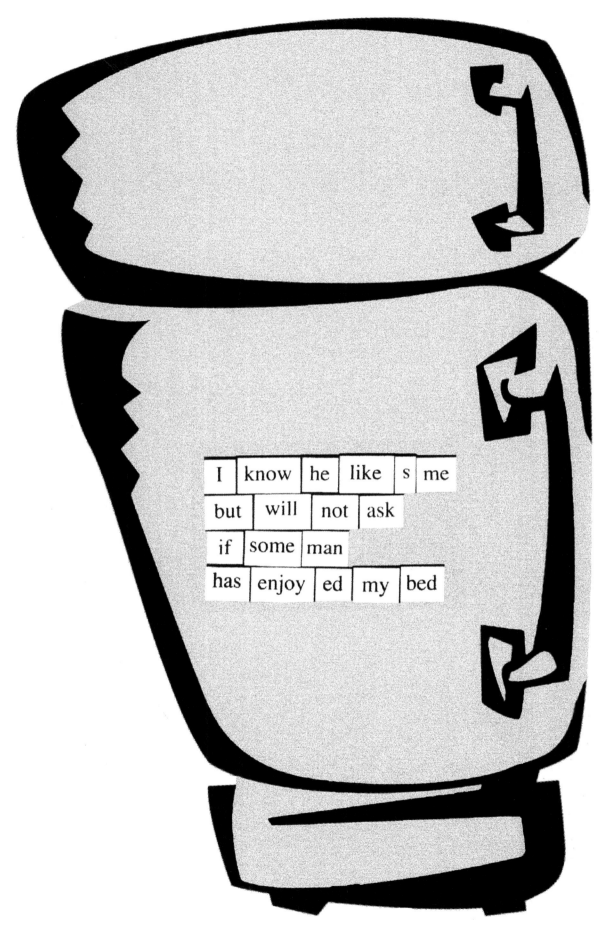

I	know	he	like	s	me
but	will	not	ask		
if	some	man			
has	enjoy	ed	my	bed	

It's peace you say
You wish for me
I have no peace with you
Every time
You come to mind
The questions start anew

Who is this man
What do you want
I no more trust in you
We are not strangers
We are not friends
You're neither vous nor tu

You left me with an imprint
On my life and in my brain
An ache
An itch
A hunger
It lingers
And won't go away

What are we then
I just don't know
A mark I can't erase
Leave me alone
Just go away
Oh how I wish you'd stay

12/1993

I have heard your voice
Filled with warmth and longing

I have seen your face
Full of expression and emotion

I have felt your touch
Strong with desire

Where is your heart
With all it's love

Where is your head
With all it's faith

Where is your soul
With all its hope

When
Will you know
Your ashes
Have risen
In Phoenix

12/1993

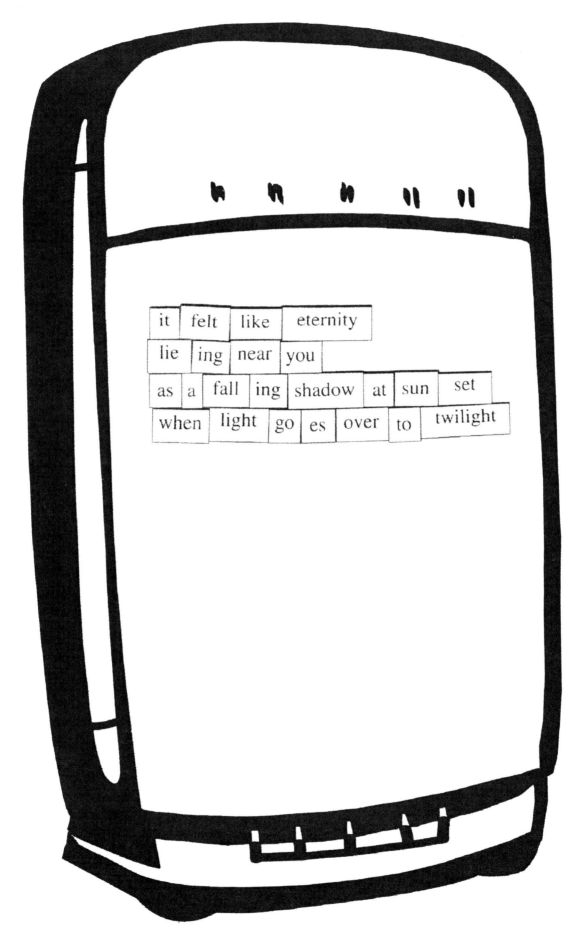

it felt like eternity
lie ing near you
as a fall ing shadow at sun set
when light go es over to twilight

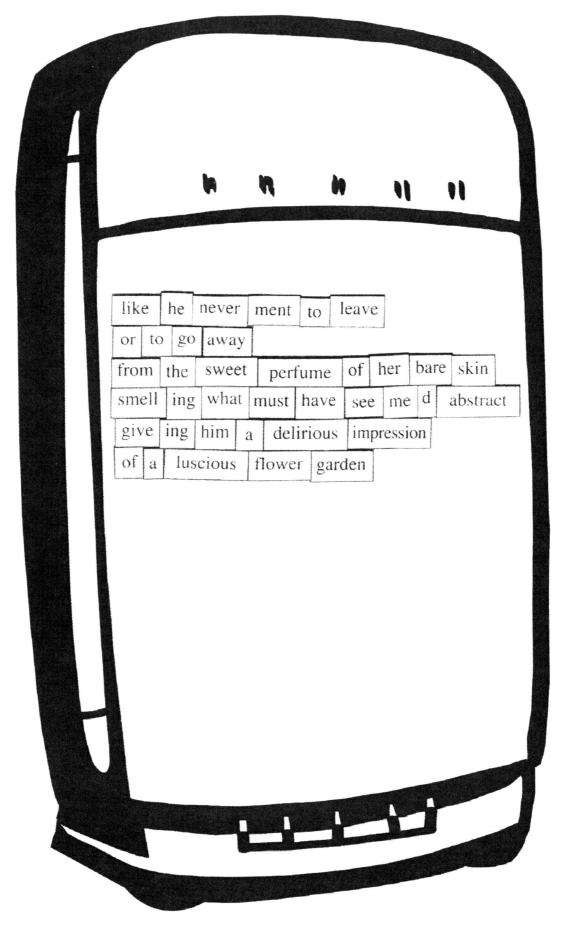

like he never ment to leave
or to go away
from the sweet perfume of her bare skin
smell ing what must have see me d abstract
give ing him a delirious impression
of a luscious flower garden

whisper essential friend

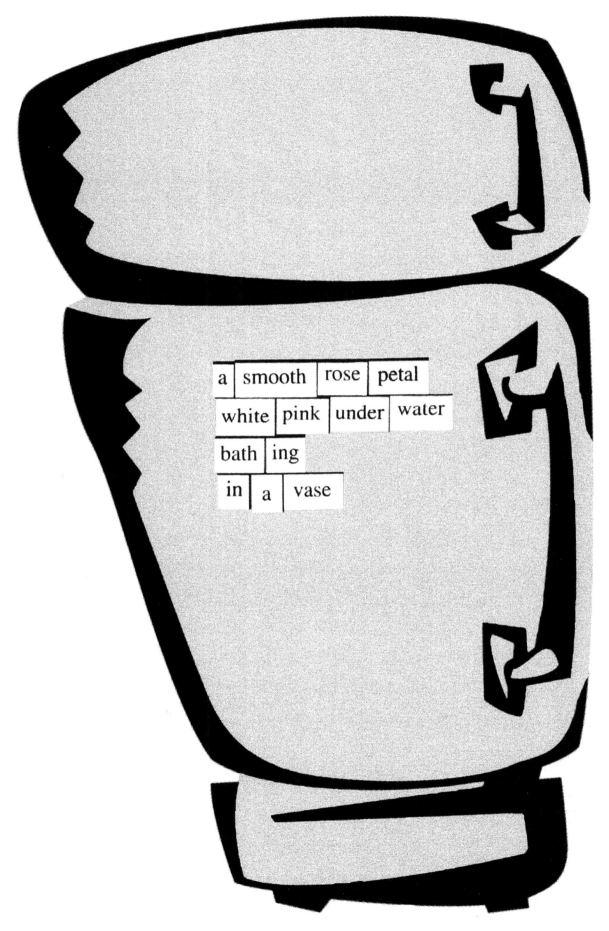

a | smooth | rose | petal
white | pink | under | water
bath | ing
in | a | vase

In pain that aches
Too much for words
Reflected in pools of darkness
Pretending to be eyes

In a heart that yearns
Too hurt to tell
To reach not
Pretending to be wanted

Surrender
Withdraw
Too near to see
Too far to say
Pretending to let go
Never having held on so tight

11/1974

whisper essential friend

here	an	d	there	
love	does		part	
but	next		ship	
dream	of	a	true	harbor

iracund

(i' rə kund') adj. prone to anger; irascible

There was an *iracund* side to Churchill that always kept his aides on guard.

Thursday	13
May	
1982	

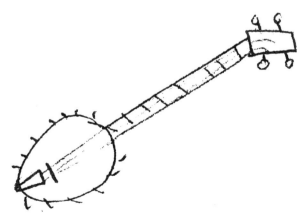

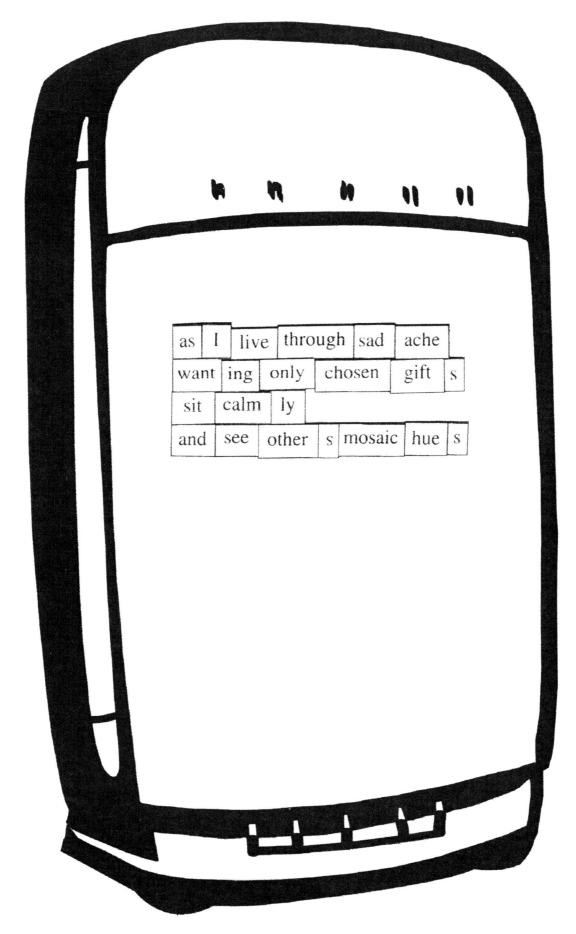

as I live through sad ache
want ing only chosen gift s
sit calm ly
and see other s mosaic hue s

paint my tapestry
a gorgeous color
red with poetry

Go to saks
Play your sax
A roll in the sack
Let's have sex

10/1997

Oh,
to be a cat.
I wish
Someone
would scratch
My head.

10/1997

Head Ache
Heart Ache
Hard on.

Headache
(Not heartache),
All gone.

08/2001

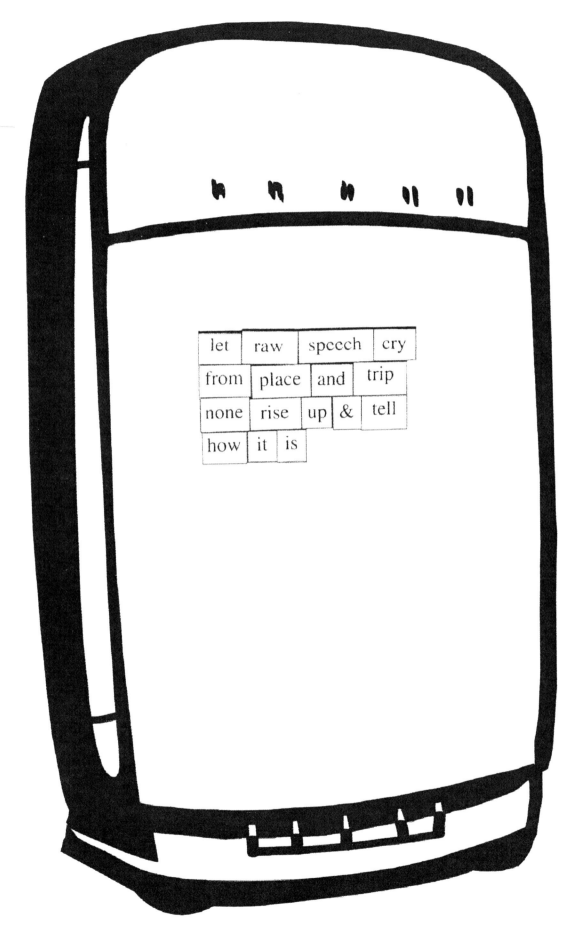

Easter

And i've seen Jesus in her eyes
The way she looks
The times she tries

The way she trembled when the preacher
Talked about faith and the birds in
the air and how they sang for god.

And i've heard silence in her song.

if we had a chance to laugh
if we had a day to breathe
if we had some ground to stand on
if we had the sea on our side

...a shouting resurrection?

And i've seen Jesus in the sky
The way he calls me
The times he tries

The way i trembled every time the
nightlight whispered me to the window
at three in the morning to see the
stars winking down

And he heard silence in my song.

Michael Hill
04/09/74

whisper essential friend

speech impediment

i

tried to carry words in bags
(to the place)
where words aren't heard but
looks converse

i

saw soft light in shadows
by a doorway i
shoved my thoughts inside
how they tumbled
(with someone)
they glanced in sentences
and sang with damp hands

i

heard piano playing and
ivory eyes dancing like keys!
songs not new
none sad or funny but calling me
behind glasses/under sheets
(the eyes have it yes and)
they shout to me from down the hall

hey!

i
tried to speak
i try to speak
words won't do where looks sing
and silence dances

Michael Hill
12/18/74

strangers in the street
haunted
betrayed
crying for stars,
greeted by the clouded sky

lured by voices
and charms
strangers in the street
secretly the same
chasing the image
of the stars
in cars
      in bedrooms
      in smoky bars
in faces, above, near the eyes
haunted

lured by hearing
"i've seen stars in some folks eyes"
betrayed
never changing,
both betrayed…
by the stars.

Michael Hill
12/19/75

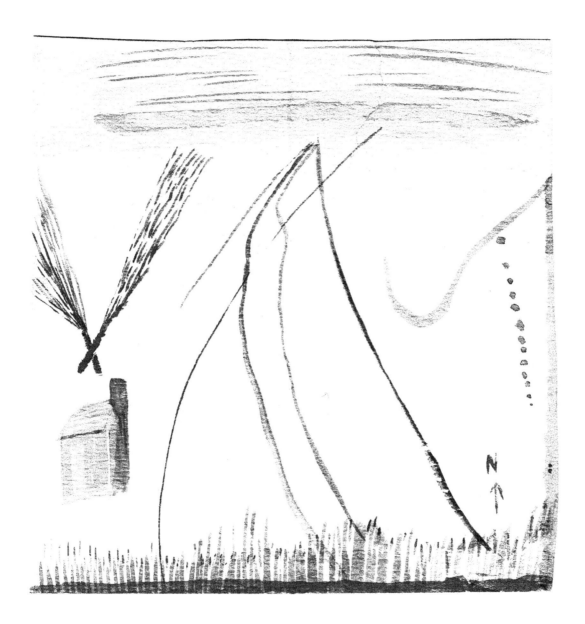

My therapist said "have faith."

My priest said "have fun."

girl be a woman

So now,

she takes her time

and spends her time

whisper essential friend

carefully.

Alone, often,

with two cats

who sleep with her

whisper essential friend

and speak volumes

with their eyes.

With gentlemen callers

that she keeps at arms length,

out of fear, out of energy,

to take another risk.

She struggles everyday to be true to herself.

She fights getting lost in the past

and caught up in the hopes of the future.

Today, she will get out …

and say a little prayer …

that perhaps she will soon discover ?

***"it was a day for small beginnings,
but who would dare despise it"***

zechariah 4:10

whisper essential friend

sea
sing
sky
say
&
worship

Acknowledgements

Thank you first and always to the good Lord for all his blessings.

Special thanks and much love to David for always being there, for the Magnetic Poetry®, The Original Kit®, and for giving me a banjo when I needed it badly.

Many thanks to Michael Hill for letting me publish his poems and watercolor painting and for being a good friend still after all these years.

Thank you to Dick for his expert advice.

I owe a huge debt of gratitude to Marilyn for the cover design, the layout assistance, and for all the guidance. I never would have published this book without her encouragement. It's a better book because of her help.

Much love to my family and friends for all their support.

love, col xo